301
TODDLER TIME
Questions & Answers

Illustrations by Michele Ackerman, Martha Avilés, Rebecca Elliot, Marina Fedotova, Daniel Howarth, Jack Hughes, Thea Kliros, Kathleen McCord, Elise Mills, Lance Raichert, and Tim Warren

Photography © Art Explosion, Artville, Brand X, Creatas, Digital Vision, Dreamstime, Image Club, iStock Photo, Jupiter Images Unlimited, Photodisc, Shutterstock, Stockbyte, and Thinkstock. © Shutterstock 2021. Gelpi (eyes: pg46, smile: pg97) Elena Fedorina (phone: pg50) Additional photography by Siede Preis Photography and Brian Warling Photography

Published by Sequoia Children's Publishing,
a division of Phoenix International Publications, Inc.

8501 West Higgins Road,
Chicago, Illinois 60631

34 Seymour Street
London W1H 7JE

Heimhuder Straße 81,
20148 Hamburg

© 2022 Sequoia Publishing & Media, LLC

Customer Service: cs@sequoiakidsbooks.com

www.SequoiaKidsBooks.com

ISBN 978-1-64269-378-2

Welcome to Active Minds!

Toddlers love to discover things and to explore the world around them. Each day presents so many opportunities for them to grow and learn. This book is one of many tools you can use to set up building blocks for early learning. This edition of Active Minds features questions about letters, numbers, colors, shapes, and new vocabulary. Singing the alphabet song, reciting nursery rhymes, and making animal noises are just some of the fun activities you and your toddler will experience in this book. Taking a few minutes a day to introduce your child to some of these early-learning concepts can have a positive impact on their development. With your help, your toddler will understand more and more of the wonderful things they see and experience every day!

How to Use

- Open to the desired set of questions.

- Read the questions aloud. Ask your child to point to or say the answer.

- Answer keys are at the back of the book.

Some Tips

- Your child might not be familiar with all of the content on these pages. Take the time to introduce new concepts and characters when questions come up.

- Encourage your child to use the book with friends and/or siblings, too. Take turns asking each other the questions. The material might serve as a good review for older children!

- Be positive and encouraging. Learning should be fun! When your child seems tired, frustrated, or unfocused, take a break. You can always play again later.

Questions

For solutions, turn to page 98.

What is this letter?

What is this tasty fruit?

What is this tiny bug?

Point to the one that begins with the letter A.

Questions

What is this letter?

B

What is this toy?

What flying animal is this?

Point to the one that begins with the letter B.

What is this letter?

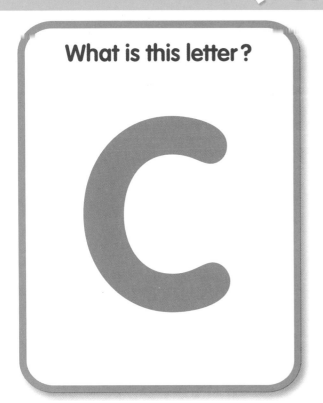

What is this furry pet?

What animal says moo?

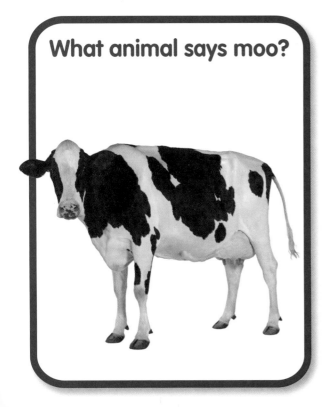

Point to the one that begins with the letter C.

Questions

What is this letter?

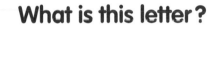

What goes quack, quack?

Who goes woof, woof?

Point to the one that begins with the letter D.

Questions

For solutions, turn to page 102.

What is this letter?

E

What do we hear with?

What is this breakfast food?

Point to the one that begins with the letter E.

What is this letter?

F

What part of the body do we use to walk?

What animal swims in the water?

Point to the one that begins with the letter F.

Questions

For solutions, turn to page 104.

What is this letter?

G

What is this farm animal?

What are these?

Point to the one that begins with the letter G.

Questions

What is this letter?

What is this?

What do you wear on your head?

Point to the one that begins with the letter H.

What is this letter?

I

What is this?

What is this cold treat?

Point to the one that begins with the letter I.

Questions

What is this letter?

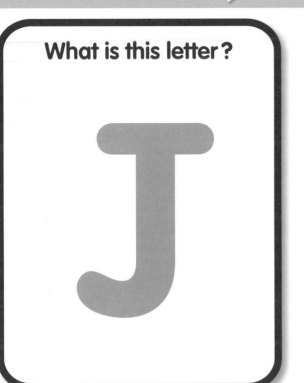

What do you wear when you go outside?

What are these?

Point to the one that begins with the letter J.

Questions

For solutions, turn to page 108.

What is this letter?

Who is wearing a crown?

What is this toy?

Point to the one that begins with the letter K.

Questions

What is this letter?

What animal is this?

What is this?

Point to the one that begins with the letter L.

Questions For solutions, turn to page 110.

What is this letter?

What is this cold drink?

What do we see in the sky at night?

Point to the one that begins with the letter M.

Questions

What is this letter?

What do you smell with?

What is this crunchy snack?

Point to the one that begins with the letter N.

Questions

For solutions, turn to page 112.

What is this letter?

What is this juicy fruit?

Who says whoo, whoo?

Point to the one that begins with the letter O.

Questions

What is this letter?

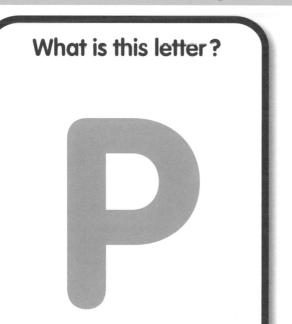

What is this crisp fruit?

Who says oink, oink?

Point to the one that begins with the letter P.

What is this letter?

Who is this person wearing a crown?

What keeps us warm?

Point to the one that begins with the letter Q.

What is this letter?

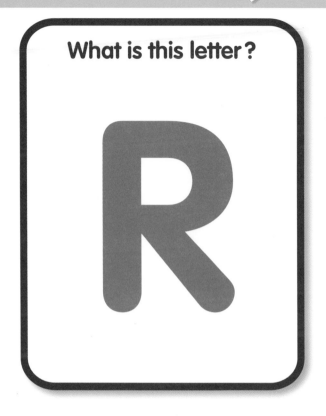

What do we use to gather up leaves?

What is this?

Point to the one that begins with the letter R.

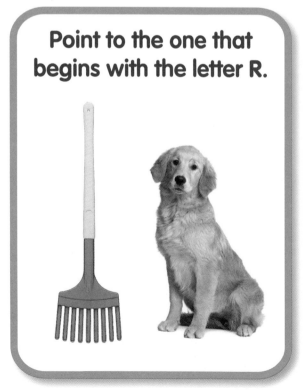

What is this letter?

S

What is big, yellow, and up in the sky?

What do we see in the sky at night?

Point to the one that begins with the letter S.

Questions

What is this letter?

T

Where can you find leaves?

What goes choo-choo?

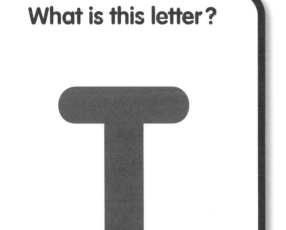

Point to the one that begins with the letter T.

Questions For solutions, turn to page 118.

What is this letter?

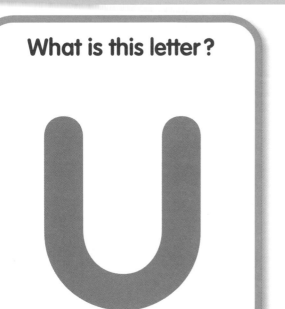

What do we use when it rains?

Which way is the arrow pointing?

Point to the one that begins with the letter U.

What is this letter?

What is this?

Where do we put flowers?

Point to the one that begins with the letter V.

What is this letter?

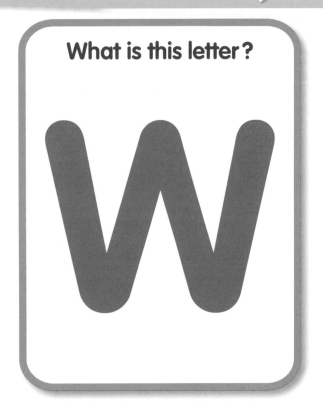

What goes around and around?

Where does a spider live?

Point to the one that begins with the letter W.

What is this letter?

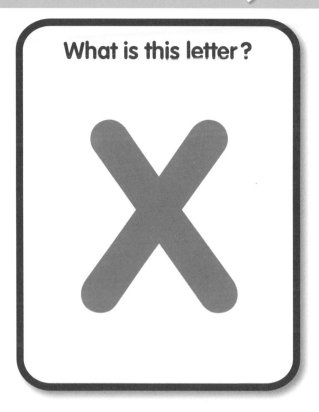

What is this?

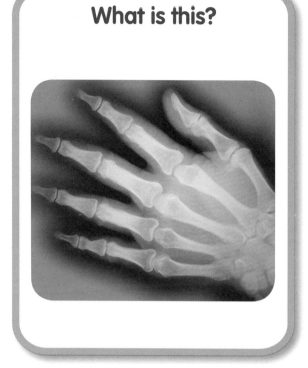

What is this instrument?

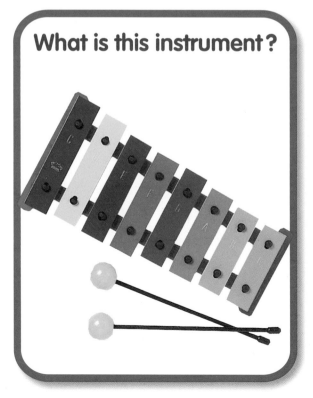

Point to the one that begins with the letter X.

What is this letter?

What is this toy?

What do we use to make sweaters?

Point to the one that begins with the letter Y.

Questions

What is this letter?

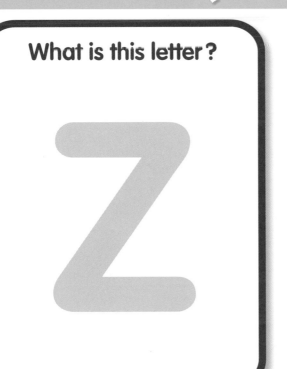

Where do we visit animals?

What is this striped animal?

Point to the one that begins with the letter Z.

Sing the Alphabet Song, then answer the questions.

A B C D E F G
H I J K
L M N O P
Q R S
T U V
W X Y Z

Now I know my ABCs! Next time, won't you sing with me?

What is the first letter of the alphabet?

What is the last letter of the alphabet?

What is this number?

1

How many birds do you see?

What is this number?

2

How many shoes do you see?

Questions

For solutions, turn to page 126.

What is this number?

3

How many mice do you see?

What is this number?

4

How many puppies do you see?

What is this number?

5

How many kittens do you see?

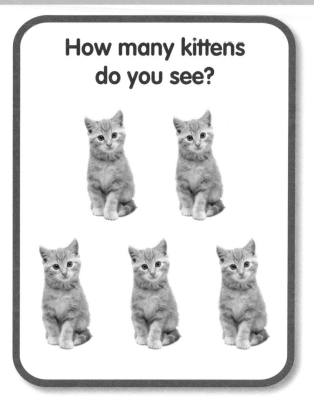

What is this number?

6

How many fish do you see?

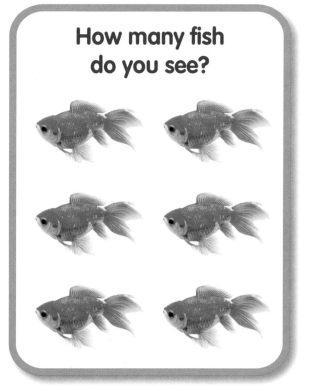

What is this number?

How many flowers do you see?

What is this number?

How many strawberries do you see?

Questions

What is this number?

9

How many balloons do you see?

What is this number?

10

How many beach balls do you see?

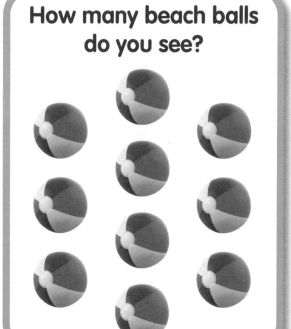

Which number is first?

1 2 3 4 5

Which number is last?

1 2 3 4 5

Questions

What color is this apple?

What color is the sun?

What color is the turtle?

What color is this ball?

Questions

For solutions, turn to page 132.

What color is this pumpkin?

What color are the grapes?

What color is this crayon?

What color is the car?

Questions

What color is the flower?

What color is this leaf?

What color is the banana?

What color is this bird?

Questions

For solutions, turn to page 134.

What is this shape?

Which one is a circle?

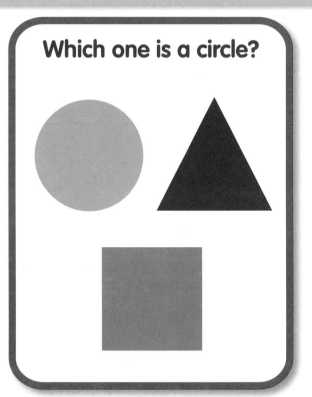

What is this shape?

Which one is a triangle?

What is this shape?

Which one is a square?

What is this shape?

Which one is a rectangle?

Questions

For solutions, turn to page 136.

Read the nursery rhyme, then answer the question.

Humpty Dumpty

Humpty Dumpty sat on a wall.
Humpty Dumpty had a great fall.
All the king's horses,
And all the king's men,
Couldn't put Humpty together again.

What happened to Humpty Dumpty?

Questions

Which one is a dog?

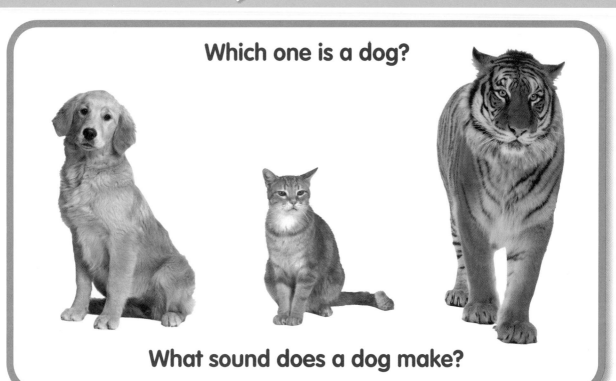

What sound does a dog make?

What is this?

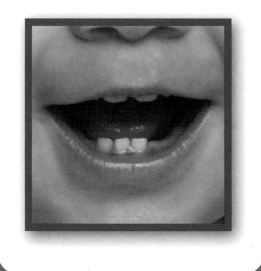

Which do we use to brush our teeth?

This animal lives in the desert. What is it called?

What is this green vegetable?

What meal comes after breakfast?

What is this tool?

Questions

Sing the song, then answer the question.

Here We Go Round the Mulberry Bush

Here we go round the mulberry bush,
The mulberry bush, the mulberry bush.
Here we go round the mulberry bush,
On a cold and frosty morning.

When do we go around the mulberry bush?

Questions

For solutions, turn to page 140.

Is the clown
happy or sad?

What are these?

Which one is a
vegetable?

People sleep in this.
What is it?

Sing the song, then answer the question.

The Ants Go Marching

The ants go marching one by one, hurrah, hurrah!
The ants go marching one by one, hurrah, hurrah!
The ants go marching one by one,
The little one stops to suck his thumb,
And they all go marching down to the ground
To get out of the rain, BOOM! BOOM! BOOM!
The ants go marching two by two, hurrah, hurrah!
The ants go marching two by two, hurrah, hurrah!
The ants go marching two by two,
The little one stops to tie his shoe,
And they all go marching down to the ground
To get out of the rain, BOOM! BOOM! BOOM!

How many purple ants do you see?

Questions
For solutions, turn to page 142.

What holiday do we dress in costumes for?

These help some people see. What are they called?

Which is the opposite of heavy?

What do we sit on to go potty?

Questions

What is this body part?

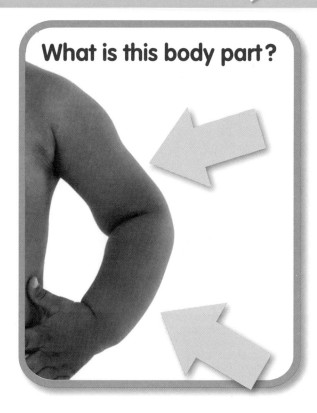

What is this red fruit?

When it's cold outside, how should we dress?

Questions

For solutions, turn to page 144.

What room would we find these in?

People talk on this. What is it?

Light comes from this. What is it?

What is this?

Which is the opposite of hot?

Which fruit is a watermelon?

What do we do before each meal?

Sing the song, then answer the question.

Twinkle Twinkle Little Star

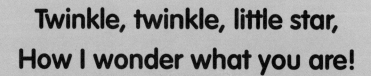

Twinkle, twinkle, little star,
How I wonder what you are.
Up above the world so high,
Like a diamond in the sky.

Twinkle, twinkle, little star,
How I wonder what you are!

Where is the star?

When do we go to bed?

On what holiday do we eat a big meal and give thanks?

What is this?

What is this sour fruit?

For solutions, turn to page 148

Read the nursery rhyme, then answer the question.

Mary's Lamb

Mary had a little lamb,
Its fleece was white as snow.
And everywhere that Mary went,
The lamb was sure to go.

What pet did Mary have?

Questions

What is this vegetable?

What are these body parts?

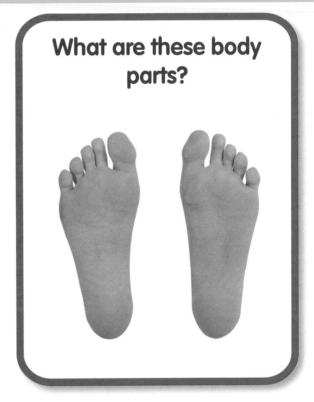

What do we use to eat?

Which is the opposite of soft?

Questions

For solutions, turn to page 150.

We sit on this. What is it?

Do we play outside at night or during the day?

What are these sweet fruits?

This animal likes cheese. What is it?

Sing the song, then answer the question.

Sing a Song of Sixpence

Sing a song of sixpence,

A pocket full of rye;

Four and twenty blackbirds

Baked in a pie!

When the pie was opened,

The birds began to sing!

Wasn't that a dainty dish

To set before the king?

What were the blackbirds baked in?

What do we wear on our feet?

What is this body part?

Which picture shows a bed?

Questions

What time of the year do flowers first bloom?

This animal is big and spends a lot of time in water. What is it?

Which do we use to clean our hands?

What do we say when we want something?

Read the nursery rhyme, then answer the question.

Rub-a-Dub-Dub

Rub-a-dub-dub,
Three men in a tub,
And how do you think they got there?
The butcher, the baker,
The candlestick-maker,
They all jumped out of a rotten potato,
'Twas enough to make a man stare.

How many men were in the tub?

Questions

Is this person mad or sad?

Which one is a carrot?

What is this part of the face?

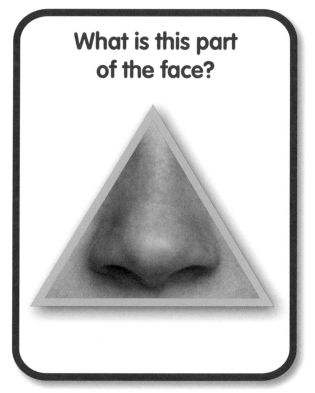

Which animal is a fish?

Sing the song, then answer the question.

BINGO

There was a farmer who had a dog,
And Bingo was his name-o.
B-I-N-G-O
B-I-N-G-O
B-I-N-G-O
And Bingo was his name-o.

Was Bingo a dog or a cat?

Questions

What is this comfy thing to sit on?

Does the picture show morning or bedtime?

This animal swings in trees. What is it?

What is this food?

Read the nursery rhyme, then answer the question.

There Was an Old Woman

There was an old woman
Who lived in a shoe.
She had so many children,
She didn't know what to do.
She gave them some broth
Without any bread.
She kissed them all sweetly
And sent them to bed.

Where did the old woman live?

Questions

What is this food?

What is this striped animal?

Where do we go to get clean?

Which would we wear to go swimming?

Sing the song, then answer the question.

Three Blind Mice

Three blind mice, three blind mice.
See how they run, see how they run!
They all ran after the farmer's wife,
Who has been afraid of mice all her life.
Did you ever think you'd see such a sight
As three blind mice?

How many mice were there?

Questions

What is this brown animal?

What is this?

What is this leafy green vegetable?

What do we say if we accidentally break something?

Questions For solutions, turn to page 162.

Read the nursery rhyme, then answer the question.

The Cat and the Fiddle

Hey diddle diddle,
The cat and the fiddle,
The cow jumped over the moon.
The little dog laughed to see such sport,
And the dish ran away with the spoon.

What did the cow jump over?

Questions

Which animal is a cat?

What sound does a cat make?

Which picture shows a playground?

Is this child mad or happy?

Sing the song, then answer the question.

The Wheels on the Bus

The wheels on the bus go round and round,
Round and round,
Round and round.
The wheels on the bus go round and round,
all through the town.

What do the wheels on the bus do?

Questions

What is this body part?

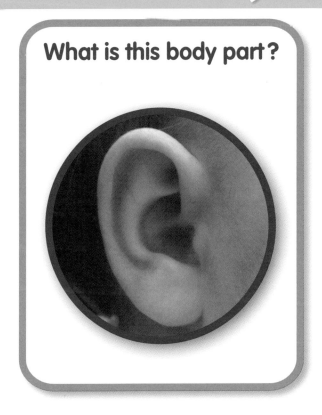

Do we say hello or goodbye when we see someone?

Which animal is a bird?

What is this vegetable?

Questions For solutions, turn to page 166.

Read the nursery rhyme, then answer the question.

Old Mother Hubbard

Old Mother Hubbard
Went to the cupboard
To give her poor dog a bone.

When she got there,
The cupboard was bare,
And so the poor dog had none.

What pet did Old Mother Hubbard have?

Questions

This tells time. What is it?

Which is the opposite of cold?

People keep food cold in here. What is it?

What do we do at night?

Sing the song, then answer the question.

If You're Happy and You Know It

If you're happy and you know it,
Clap your hands!
If you're happy and you know it,
Clap your hands!
If you're happy and you know it,
And you really want to show it,
If you're happy and you know it,
Clap your hands!

If you're happy and you know it, what should you do?

What is this child doing?

We can ride this animal. What is it?

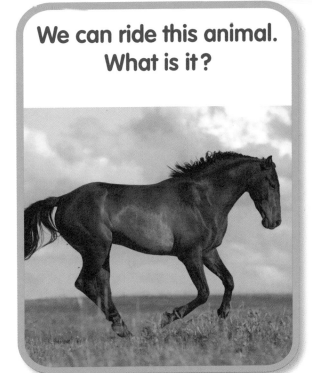

What is this yellow fruit?

What holiday in July do we celebrate with fireworks?

Read the nursery rhyme, then answer the question.

Little Miss Muffet

Little Miss Muffet
Sat on a tuffet,
Eating her curds and whey.

Then along came a spider,
Who sat down beside her
And frightened Miss Muffet away.

What frightened Little Miss Muffet?

Questions

What is this?

Which picture shows snow?

This animal hops. What is it?

What is this sweet fruit?

Sing the song, then answer the question.

Itsy Bitsy Spider

The itsy bitsy spider crawled up the water spout.
Down came the rain, and washed the spider out.
Out came the sun, and dried up all the rain,
and the itsy bitsy spider went up the spout again.

What dried up all the rain?

Questions

People watch shows on this. What is it?

Is it dark outside in the morning or at night?

What room is the child in?

We rest our heads on this. What is it?

Read the nursery rhyme, then answer the question.

Jack and Jill

Jack and Jill went up the hill,
To fetch a pail of water.
Jack fell down and broke his crown,
And Jill came tumbling after.

Who went up the hill?

Questions

What is the opposite of wet?

We read these. What are they called?

Which do we wear outside if it's raining?

What holiday is celebrated with hearts and candy?

Questions

For solution, turn to page 176.

Sing the song, then answer the question.

Row, Row, Row Your Boat

Row, row, row your boat,

Gently down the stream.

Merrily, merrily, merrily, merrily,

Life is but a dream.

Which one is a boat?

Questions

Where is the car parked?

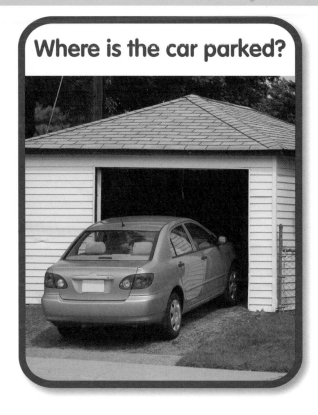

What do we wear to keep our hands warm?

Which picture looks like it's warm outside?

What is this food we use to make sandwiches?

For solution, turn to page 178.

Read the nursery rhyme, then answer the question.

Pat-a-Cake

Pat-a-cake, pat-a-cake,

Baker's man.

Bake me a cake

As fast as you can.

Roll it, and pat it,

And mark it with a B,

Put it in the oven for baby and me!

What was the cake marked with?

Questions

What do we say when we are leaving?

Where do people cook food?

Which is the opposite of loud?

Where would we find the potty?

Questions

For solution, turn to page 180.

This is something we wear. What is it called?

People drive this. What is it?

Which picture shows the morning?

What fruit has a spiky outside?

Sing the song, then answer the question.

Pop! Goes the Weasel

All around the cobbler's bench
The monkey chased the weasel.
The monkey thought it was all in fun,
Pop! Goes the weasel.

Which one is a monkey?

Questions

For solution, turn to page 182.

What should we say when someone gives us a gift?

What is this food?

When do leaves fall off the trees?

What is this body part?

Read the nursery rhyme, then answer the question.

Hickory Dickory Dock

Hickory, dickory, dock,
The mouse ran up the clock.
The clock struck one,
The mouse ran down,
Hickory, dickory, dock.

Where did the mouse run?

Questions

For solutions, turn to page 184.

What season is it when we swim outside?

What is this yummy snack?

What is the child eating?

When do we eat breakfast?

Questions

Sing the song, then answer the question.

London Bridge

London Bridge is falling down,

Falling down, falling down.

London Bridge is falling down,

My fair lady.

What is happening to London Bridge?

What comes next?

Who puts out fires?

What animal is this?

Which is the opposite of day?

Questions

What shape is this?

What fruit is this?

Which one belongs in a bedroom?

Which apple is red?

What number comes after 1?

1 ? 3

What is the child eating?

How many baseballs are there?

What letter comes after A?

A ? C

Questions

How many ears do we have?

Which one is a blue circle?

Which one is a triangle?

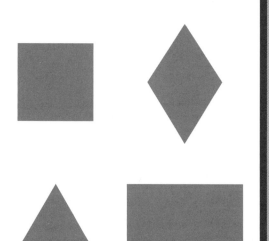

Which crayon is red?

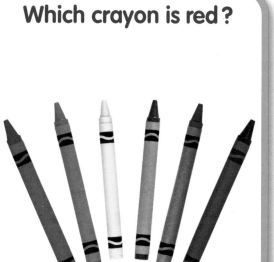

Which person is happy?

How many fingers do we have?

What number comes next?

1 2 ?

We see a doctor when we are sick. Which one is a doctor?

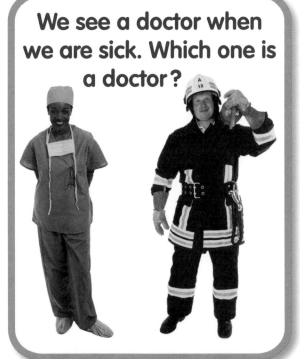

Questions

Which one is a green rectangle?

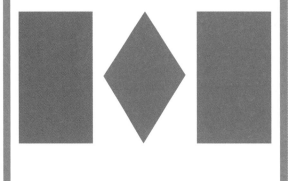

What number comes after 9?

8 9 ?

What do we smile with?

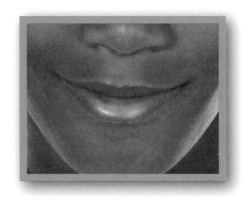

Which should we never touch?

What is this letter?
This is the letter A.

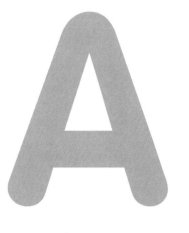

What is this tasty fruit?
Apple

What is this tiny bug?
Ant

Point to the one that
begins with the letter A.
Apple

What is this letter?
This is the letter B.

B

What is this toy?
Ball

What flying animal is this?
Bat

Point to the one that begins with the letter B.

Ball

Answers for page 6

What is this letter?
This is the letter C.

What is this furry pet?
Cat

What animal says moo?
Cow

Point to the one that
begins with the letter C.

Cat

What is this letter?
This is the letter D.

D

What goes quack, quack?
Duck

Who goes woof, woof?
Dog

Point to the one that begins with the letter D.

Duck

Answers for page 8

What is this letter?

This is the letter E.

E

What do we hear with?

Ear

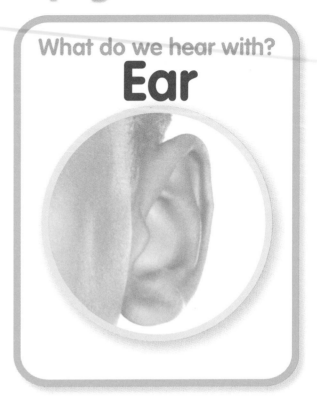

What is this breakfast food?

Egg

Point to the one that begins with the letter E.

Egg

What is this letter?

This is the letter F.

F

What part of the body do we use to walk?

Feet

What animal swims in the water?

Fish

Point to the one that begins with the letter F.

Fish

Answers for page 10

What is this letter?
This is the letter G.

What is this farm animal?
Goat

What are these?
Grapes

Point to the one that
begins with the letter G.

Goat

What is this letter?

This is the letter H.

H

What is this?

House

What do you wear
on your head?

Hat

Point to the one that
begins with the letter H.

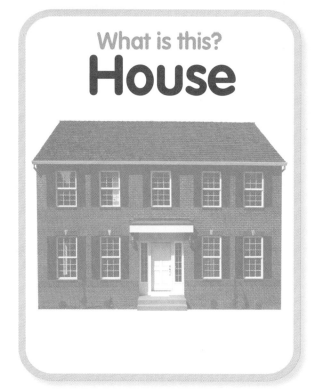

House

What is this letter?
This is the letter I.

I

What is this?
Ice

What is this cold treat?
Ice cream

Point to the one that begins with the letter I.

Ice

What is this letter?

This is the letter J.

J

What do you wear when you go outside?

Jacket

What are these?

Jelly beans

Point to the one that begins with the letter J.

Jelly beans

What is this letter?
This is the letter K.

Who is wearing a crown?
King

What is this toy?
Kite

Point to the one that begins with the letter K.
King

What is this letter?
This is the letter L.

L

What animal is this?
Lion

What is this?
Leaf

Point to the one that begins with the letter L.

Leaf

What is this letter?
This is the letter M.

What is this cold drink?

Milk

What do we see in the sky at night?

Moon

Point to the one that begins with the letter M.

Milk

What is this letter?

This is the letter N.

N

What do you smell with?

Nose

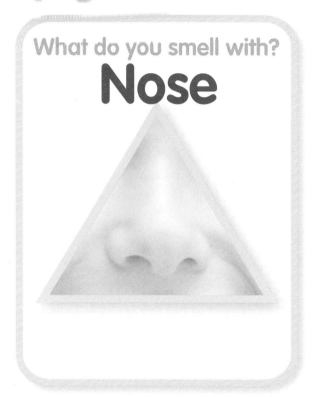

What is this crunchy snack?

Nuts

Point to the one that begins with the letter N.

Nuts

What is this letter?
This is the letter O.

What is this juicy fruit?
Orange

Who says whoo, whoo?
Owl

Point to the one that begins with the letter O.
Orange

What is this letter?
This is the letter P.

P

What is this crisp fruit?
Pear

Who says oink, oink?
Pig

Point to the one that begins with the letter P.
Pear

What is this letter?
This is the letter Q.

Q

Who is this person wearing a crown?

Queen

What keeps us warm?
Quilt

Point to the one that begins with the letter Q.

Queen

What is this letter?
This is the letter R.

R

What do we use to
gather up leaves?
Rake

What is this?
Rainbow

Point to the one that
begins with the letter R.
Rake

What is this letter?
This is the letter S.

What is big, yellow, and up in the sky?

Sun

What do we see in the sky at night?

Stars

Point to the one that begins with the letter S.

Sun

What is this letter?

This is the letter T.

T

Where can you find leaves?

Tree

What goes choo-choo?

Train

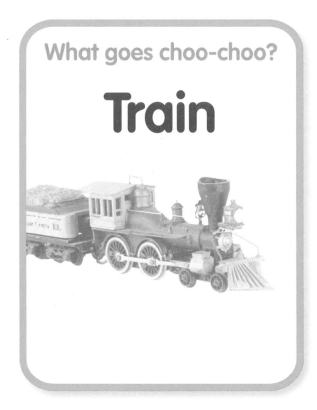

Point to the one that begins with the letter T.

Tree

What is this letter?
This is the letter U.

What do we use
when it rains?
Umbrella

Which way is the
arrow pointing?
Up

Point to the one that
begins with the letter U.

Umbrella

What is this letter?
This is the letter V.

What is this?
Vest

Where do we put flowers?
Vase

Point to the one that begins with the letter V.

Vase

What is this letter?
This is the letter W.

W

What goes around and around?
Wheel

Where does a spider live?
Web

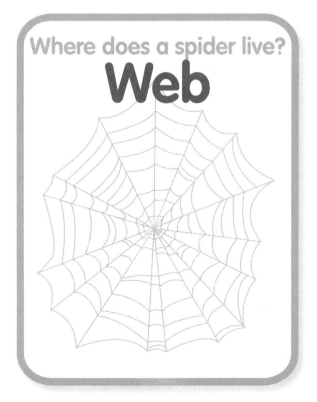

Point to the one that begins with the letter W.

Wheel

What is this letter?

This is the letter X.

What is this?

X-ray

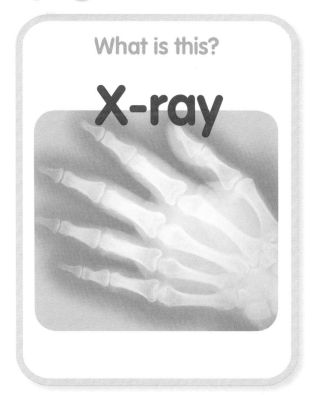

What is this instrument?

Xylophone

Point to the one that begins with the letter X.

X-ray

What is this letter?

This is the letter Y.

What is this toy?

Yo-yo

What do we use to make sweaters?

Yarn

Point to the one that begins with the letter Y.

Yarn

What is this letter?
This is the letter Z.

Z

Where do we visit animals?

Zoo

What is this striped animal?

Zebra

Point to the one that begins with the letter Z.

Zebra

Sing the Alphabet Song, then answer the questions.

A is the first letter of the alphabet.

Z is the last letter of the alphabet.

Now I know my ABCs! Next time, won't you sing with me?

What is the first letter of the alphabet?

What is the last letter of the alphabet?

What is this number?

1

This is the number 1.

How many birds do you see?

1

What is this number?

2

This is the number 2.

How many shoes do you see?

2

Answers for page 32

What is this number?

3

This is the number 3.

How many mice do you see?

What is this number?

4

This is the number 4.

How many puppies do you see?

What is this number?

5

This is the number 5.

How many kittens do you see?

What is this number?

6

This is the number 6.

How many fish do you see?

Answers for page 34

What is this number?

7

This is the number 7.

How many flowers do you see?

What is this number?

8

This is the number 8.

How many strawberries do you see?

What is this number?

9

This is the number 9.

How many balloons do you see?

What is this number?

10

This is the number 10.

How many beach balls do you see?

Answers for page 36

Which number is first?

1 2 3 4 5

Which number is last?

1 2 3 4 5

What color is this apple?

This apple is red.

What color is the sun?

Yellow

What color is the turtle?

Green

What color is this ball?

This ball is orange.

What color is this pumpkin?

Orange

What color are the grapes?

The grapes are purple.

What color is this crayon?

This crayon is blue.

What color is the car?

Red

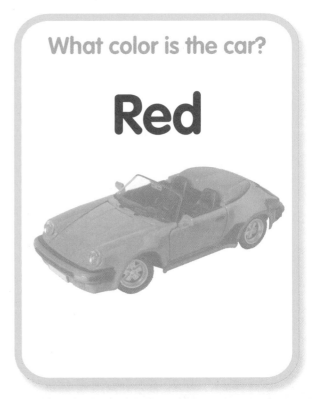

What color is the flower?
Purple

What color is this leaf?

This leaf is green.

What color is the banana?

The banana is yellow.

What color is this bird?

Blue

What is this shape?

Circle

Which one is a circle?

This is a circle.

What is this shape?

Triangle

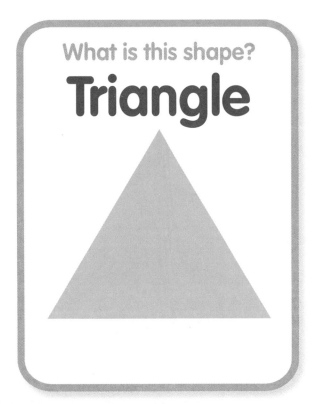

Which one is a triangle?

This is a triangle.

What is this shape?

Square

Which one is a square?

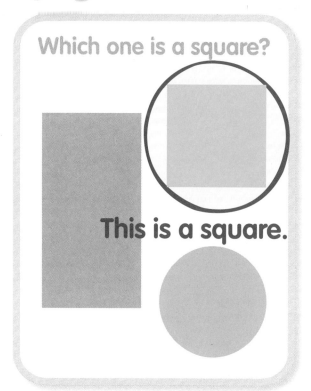

This is a square.

What is this shape?

Rectangle

Which one is a rectangle?

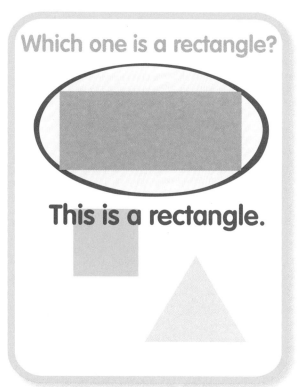

This is a rectangle.

Answers for page 42

Read the nursery rhyme, then answer the question.

Humpty Dumpty

Humpty Dumpty sat on a wall.
Humpty Dumpty had a great fall.
All the king's horses,
And all the king's men,
Couldn't put Humpty together again.

What happened to Humpty Dumpty?

Which one is a dog?

Woof

What sound does a dog make?

What is this?
Mouth

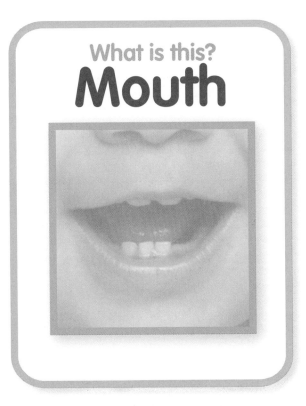

Which do we use to brush our teeth?
Toothbrush

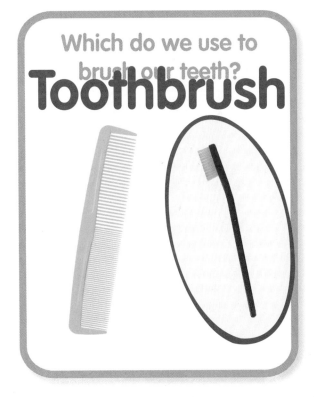

This animal lives in the desert. What is it called?

Camel

What is this green vegetable?

Broccoli

What meal comes after breakfast?

Lunch

What is this tool?

Hammer

Sing the song, then answer the question.

Here We Go Round the Mulberry Bush

Here we go round the mulberry bush,
The mulberry bush, the mulberry bush.
Here we go round the mulberry bush,
On a cold and frosty morning.

When do we go around the mulberry bush?

Is the clown happy or **sad**?

What are these?

Eyes

Which one is a vegetable?

People sleep in this. What is it?

Bed

Sing the song, then answer the question.

The Ants Go Marching

The ants go marching one by one, hurrah, hurrah!
The ants go marching one by one, hurrah, hurrah!
The ants go marching one by one,
The little one stops to suck his thumb,
And they all go marching down to the ground
To get out of the rain, BOOM! BOOM! BOOM!
The ants go marching two by two, hurrah, hurrah!
The ants go marching two by two, hurrah, hurrah!
The ants go marching two by two,
The little one stops to tie his shoe,
And they all go marching down to the ground
To get out of the rain, BOOM! BOOM! BOOM!

How many purple ants do you see?

3

What holiday do we dress in costumes for?

Halloween

These help some people see. What are they called?

Glasses

Which is the opposite of heavy?

Light

What do we sit on to go potty?

Toilet

Answers for page 49

What is this body part?

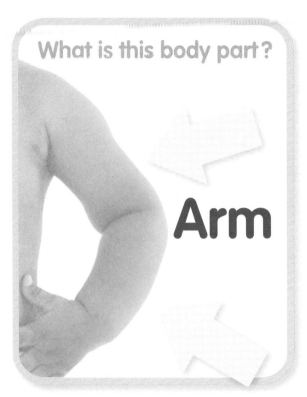

Arm

What is this red fruit?

Strawberry

When it's cold outside, how should we dress?

What room would we find these in?

Kitchen

People talk on this. What is it?

Telephone

Light comes from this. What is it?

Lamp

What is this?

Computer

Which is the opposite of hot?

Cold

Which fruit is a watermelon?

What do we do before each meal?

Wash our hands

Sing the song, then answer the question.

Twinkle Twinkle Little Star

Twinkle, twinkle, little star,
How I wonder what you are.
Up above the world so high,
Like a diamond in the sky.

Twinkle, twinkle, little star,
How I wonder what you are!

Where is the star?

When do we go to bed?

Night

On what holiday do we eat a big meal and give thanks?

Thanksgiving

What is this?

Toothbrush

What is this sour fruit?

Lemon

Read the nursery rhyme, then answer the question.

Mary's Lamb

Mary had a little lamb,
Its fleece was white as snow.
And everywhere that Mary went,
The lamb was sure to go.

What pet did Mary have?

What is this vegetable?

Corn

What are these body parts?

Feet

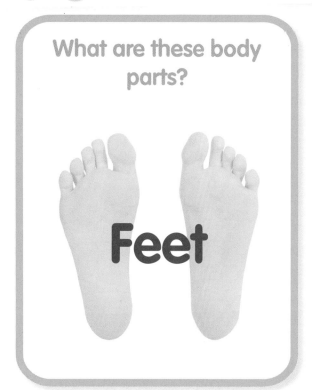

What do we use to eat?

Spoon

Which is the opposite of soft?

Hard

We sit on this. What is it?

Chair

Do we play outside at night or (during the day)?

What are these sweet fruits?
Grapes

This animal likes cheese. What is it?
Mouse

Sing the song, then answer the question.

Sing a Song of Sixpence

Sing a song of sixpence,

A pocket full of rye;

Four and twenty blackbirds

Baked in a pie!

When the pie was opened,

The birds began to sing!

Wasn't that a dainty dish

To set before the king?

What were the blackbirds baked in?

Answers for page 58

What do we wear on our feet?

Shoes

What is this body part?

Leg

Which picture shows a bed?

What time of the year do flowers first bloom?

Spring

This animal is big and spends a lot of time in water. What is it?

Hippo

Which do we use to clean our hands?

What do we say when we want something?

Please

Read the nursery rhyme, then answer the question.

Rub-a-Dub-Dub

Rub-a-dub-dub,

Three men in a tub,

And how do you think they got there?

The butcher, the baker,

The candlestick-maker,

They all jumped out of a rotten potato,

'Twas enough to make a man stare.

How many men were in the tub?

Is this person **mad** or sad?

Which one is a carrot?

What is this part
of the face?

Nose

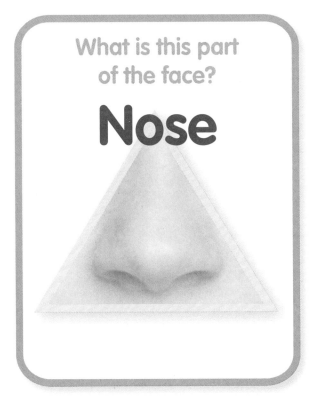

Which animal is a fish?

Sing the song, then answer the question.

BINGO

There was a farmer who had a **dog**,

And Bingo was his name-o.

B-I-N-G-O

B-I-N-G-O

B-I-N-G-O

And Bingo was his name-o.

Was Bingo a dog or a cat?

What is this comfy thing to sit on?

Couch
or
Sofa

Does the picture show (morning) or bedtime?

This animal swings in trees. What is it?

Monkey

What is this food?

Tomato

Read the nursery rhyme, then answer the question.

There Was an Old Woman

There was an old woman
Who lived **in a shoe**.
She had so many children,
She didn't know what to do.
She gave them some broth
Without any bread.
She kissed them all sweetly
And sent them to bed.

Where did the old woman live?

What is this food?

Hot dog

What is this striped animal?

Tiger

Where do we go to get clean?

Bathtub

Which would we wear to go swimming?

Sing the song, then answer the question.

Three Blind Mice

Three blind mice, three blind mice.
See how they run, see how they run!
They all ran after the farmer's wife,
Who has been afraid of mice all her life.
Did you ever think you'd see such a sight
As three blind mice?

How many mice were there?

What is this brown animal?

Bear

What is this?

Sandwich

What is this leafy green vegetable?

Lettuce

What do we say if we accidentally break something?

I'm Sorry

Read the nursery rhyme, then answer the question.

The Cat and the Fiddle

Hey diddle diddle,
The cat and the fiddle,
The cow jumped over the moon.
The little dog laughed to see such sport,
And the dish ran away with the spoon.

What did the cow jump over?

Which animal is a cat?

Meow

What sound does a cat make?

Which picture shows
a playground?

Is this child
mad or happy?

Sing the song, then answer the question.

The Wheels on the Bus

The wheels on the bus go round and round,
Round and Round,
Round and Round.
The wheels on the bus go round and round,
all through the town.

What do the wheels on the bus do?

What is this body part?

Ear

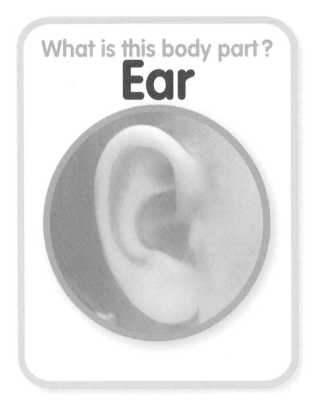

Do we say hello or goodbye when we see someone?

Which animal is a bird?

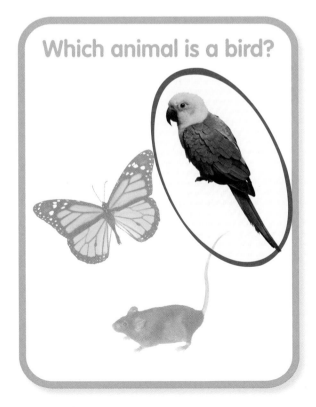

What is this vegetable?

Potato

Read the nursery rhyme, then answer the question.

Old Mother Hubbard

Old Mother Hubbard
Went to the cupboard
To give her poor **dog** a bone.

When she got there,
The cupboard was bare,
And so the poor dog had none.

What pet did Old Mother Hubbard have?

This tells time. What is it?

Clock

Which is the opposite of cold?

Hot

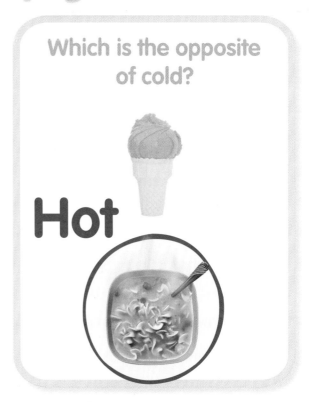

People keep food cold in here. What is it?

Refrigerator

What do we do at night?

Sleep

Sing the song, then answer the question.

If You're Happy and You Know It

If you're happy and you know it,
Clap your hands!
If you're happy and you know it,
Clap your hands!
If you're happy and you know it,
And you really want to show it,
If you're happy and you know it,
Clap your hands!

If you're happy and you know it, what should you do?

What is this child doing?
Brushing his hair

We can ride this animal.
What is it?
Horse

What is this yellow fruit?
Banana

What holiday in July
do we celebrate with
fireworks?
Fourth of July

Answer for page 76

Read the nursery rhyme, then answer the question.

Little Miss Muffet

Little Miss Muffet
Sat on a tuffet,
Eating her curds and whey.

Then along came **a spider**,
Who sat down beside her
And frightened Miss Muffet away.

What frightened Little Miss Muffet?

What is this?

Table

Which picture shows snow?

This animal hops. What is it?

Bunny

What is this sweet fruit?

Cherry

Answer for page 78

Sing the song, then answer the question.

Itsy Bitsy Spider

The itsy bitsy spider crawled up the water spout.
Down came the rain, and washed the spider out.
Out came **the sun**, and dried up all the rain,
and the itsy bitsy spider went up the spout again.

What dried up all the rain?

People watch shows on this. What is it?

Television

Is it dark outside in the morning or (at night)?

What room is the child in?

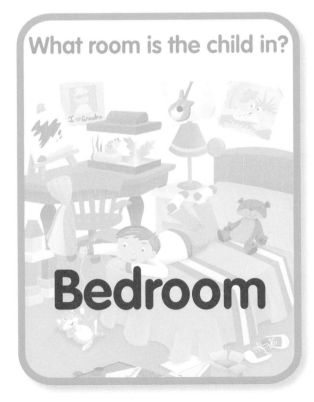

Bedroom

We rest our heads on this. What is it?

Pillow

Answer for page 80

Read the nursery rhyme, then answer the question.

Jack and Jill

Jack and Jill went up the hill,
To fetch a pail of water.
Jack fell down and broke his crown,
And Jill came tumbling after.

Who went up the hill?

What is the opposite
of wet?

Dry

We read these.
What are they called?

Books

Which do we wear outside
if it's raining?

Raincoat

What holiday is
celebrated with hearts
and candy?

Valentine's Day

Answer for page 82

Sing the song, then answer the question.

Row, Row, Row Your Boat

Row, row, row your boat,

Gently down the stream.

Merrily, merrily, merrily, merrily,

Life is but a dream.

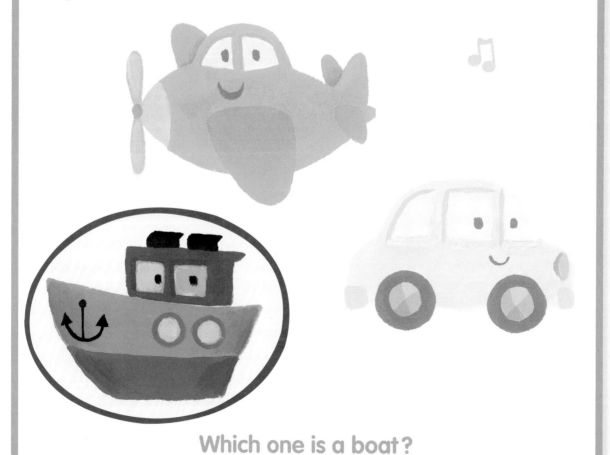

Which one is a boat?

Where is the car parked?

Garage

What do we wear to keep our hands warm?

Gloves

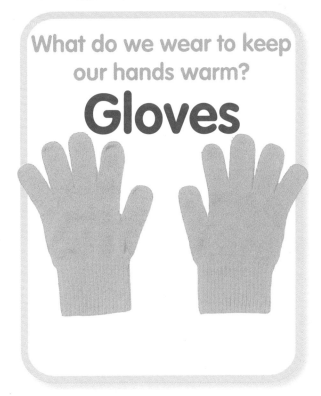

Which picture looks like it's warm outside?

What is this food we use to make sandwiches?

Bread

Read the nursery rhyme, then answer the question.

Pat-a-Cake

Pat-a-cake, pat-a-cake,

Baker's man.

Bake me a cake

As fast as you can.

Roll it, and pat it,

And mark it **with a B**,

Put it in the oven for baby and me!

What was the cake marked with?

What do we say when we are leaving?

Bye-bye

Where do people cook food?

Kitchen

Which is the opposite of loud?

Quiet

Where would we find the potty?

Bathroom

Answer for page 86

This is something we wear. What is it called?

People drive this. What is it?

Car

Which picture shows the morning?

What fruit has a spiky outside?

Pineapple

Sing the song, then answer the question.

Pop! Goes the Weasel

All around the cobbler's bench
The monkey chased the weasel.
The monkey thought it was all in fun,
Pop! Goes the weasel.

Which one is a monkey?

What should we say when someone gives us a gift?

Thank you

What is this food?

Cheese

When do leaves fall off the trees?

In the Fall

What is this body part?

Hand

Read the nursery rhyme, then answer the question.

Hickory Dickory Dock

Hickory, dickory, dock,

The mouse ran up the clock.

The clock struck one,

The mouse ran down,

Hickory, dickory, dock.

Where did the mouse run?

What season is it when we swim outside?
Summer

What is this yummy snack?
Crackers

What is the child eating?
Pizza

When do we eat breakfast?
Morning

Sing the song, then answer the question.

London Bridge

London Bridge is falling down,
Falling down, falling down.
London Bridge is falling down,
My fair lady.

What is happening to London Bridge?

What comes next?

Who puts out fires?

Firefighter

What animal is this?

Giraffe

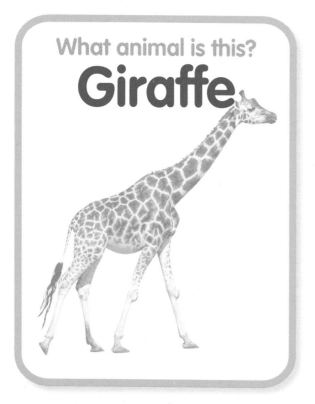

Which is the opposite of day?

Night

What shape is this?
Oval

What fruit is this?
Peach

Which one belongs in a bedroom?

Which apple is red?

What number comes after 1?

1 2 3

What is the child eating?

Spaghetti

How many baseballs are there?

4

What letter comes after A?

A B C

How many ears do we have?

2

Which one is a blue circle?

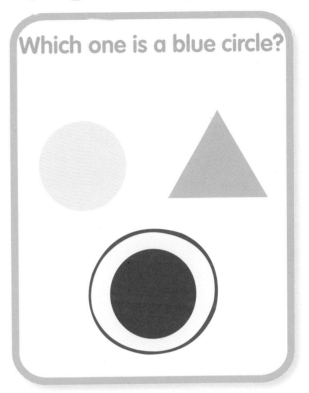

Which one is a triangle?

Which crayon is red?

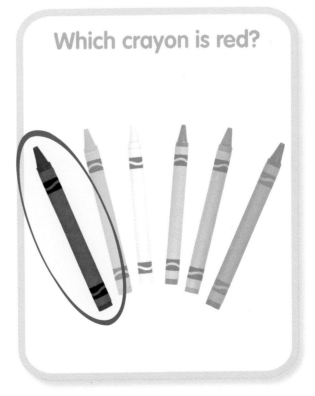

Which person is happy?

How many fingers do we have?

What number comes next?

1 2 3

We see a doctor when we are sick. Which one is a doctor?

Which one is a green rectangle?

What number comes after 9?

8 9 10

What do we smile with?

Mouth

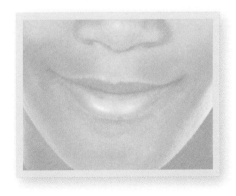

Which should we never touch?

CONGRATULATIONS!

YOU DID IT!